Hi, My Name is Jett:

AUTISM IN SCHOOL

Written by
Michelle Jennings

Illustrated by
Michelle Beasley

AuthorHouse™
1663 Liberty Drive
Bloomington, IN 47403
www.authorhouse.com
Phone: 1-800-839-8640

First published by AuthorHouse 06/13/2011
ISBN: 978-1-4634-2656-9 (sc)

Library of Congress Control Number: 2011910063

Printed in the United States of America

This book is printed on acid-free paper.

Because of the dynamic nature of the Internet, any web addresses or links contained in this book may have changed since publication and may no longer be valid. The views expressed in this work are solely those of the author and do not necessarily reflect the views of the publisher, and the publisher hereby disclaims any responsibility for them.

authorHOUSE®

For my son, Jett, the educators and "special teachers" who have worked to help him acclimate to all the elements of being a successful student. I firmly believe that your patience and efforts collaborated to provide my son and I with the best possible tools necessary to ensure that he excels in his educational career. I can never thank you enough.

Miss Libby, Miss Angie, Miss Peggy, Miss Trish, Mrs. Lilly, Mrs. Z., Mrs. McAtee, Ms. Robbins, Mrs. Redden, Miss Brenda, Mrs. Mortimer, Mrs. Weishaar, Miss S. and Miss Taylor

Since Jett's diagnosis, it has been a constant search for knowledge, resources and answers.

I attended my first Autism conference in June 2008 with my Mom, where I took 42 pages of notes. It certainly jump-started my journey into learning about the world my son is in, and my Mom says while it was a bit overwhelming at first, she is so glad she went, she feels like she can better connect with and understand her oldest grandchild.

The Autism ribbon is comprised of puzzle pieces. It was explained to me that "the spectrum" is so wide, it's like a 10,000-piece puzzle. Each child on the spectrum is comprised of only 10 pieces, and it is our job as parents to find which 10 pieces make up our own child. The pieces that I have uncovered so far about Jett's Autism I could not have done without the help of the teachers he has been so fortunate to have. Every day I look for signs that we're just a little bit closer to recovering Jett and pulling him through that preverbal window, and every day I thank God for entrusting this beautiful angel to me.

Hi, my name is Jett, and I have *Autism*. I have some special needs that make me different, but there are also a lot of things about me that are the same as other kids, too.

In the summer, my school counselor made me a *social story book*. There are pictures of the bus, classrooms and teachers. Mama reads it to me every night during bath time before the school year starts.

I get to go to school on the bus. Mama walks me to the bus and reminds me to say 'Good morning' to the bus driver. It's important to be polite.

The bus driver helps me put my seatbelt on. I get to sit in the first seat right behind her. Sometimes I forget to say 'Thank you'. It's hard to remember my words all the time.

I like riding the bus, it's very bumpy. The vibration relaxes me. Normally, I have a hard time sitting still in chairs, but I'm an excellent rider. I also like to look out of the window.

When the bus gets to school, my special teacher is waiting for me at the door. She is called a Para. She is part of my IEP (Individual Education Plan) Team. She uses short sentences and visual aids. She helps me all day and also writes daily to Mama in my journal.

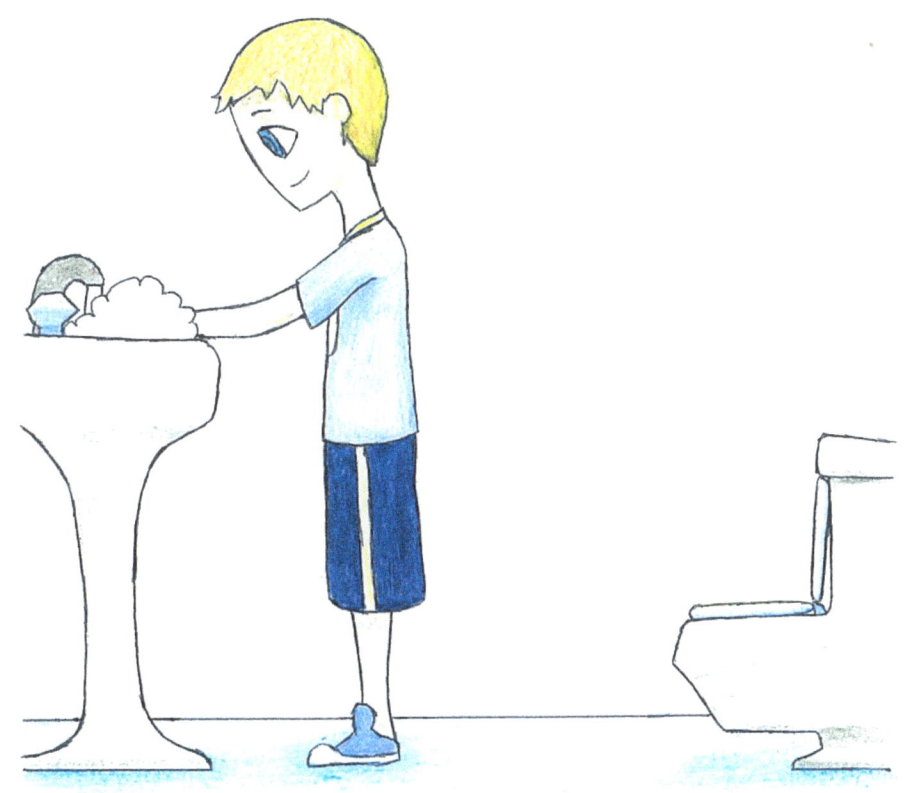

In the restroom, sometimes I need help with my pants. I wash my hands pretty good, but the hand dryer is very loud. Sometimes I put my hands over my ears.

In my classroom, I have a *visual schedule*. It's easier for me to understand things I can see. There are pictures on my schedule that show me what we'll be doing and what order we'll do them. There are also picture cards that I can use to tell my Para when I need a break. I have a hard time with sudden changes in schedules.

Sometimes I need to take a break from my classroom. When there's too much noise, or I don't get to move around, I may start hitting or biting myself, screaming or kicking. My Para takes me to the *Sensory Room* to calm down.

Many people are on my IEP Team. Some days I work with an O.T. (*Occupational Therapist.*) She teaches me to use a pencil, crayons, scissors and other classroom tools. Every day I also work with an *Autism Consultant.* I need to learn how to behave with my friends.

Some days my class goes to the gym for **P.E.** I like moving around. It is hard for me to listen and follow directions because it can get pretty loud. My Para may have to take me to the **Sensory Room.**

Other days we get to sing or play instruments in Music class. I like music, and I enjoy getting to play different instruments with my classmates, but again, sometimes it can be too loud for me. A sure sign is when I put my hands over my ears.

My school let's my class go to lunch first so it's not loud when I walk in. Eating at school is a lot different than eating at home. I don't have my Para, so I tap my hands and swing my feet a lot to block out all the noise.

Some days we go to another classroom filled with bright colors and fun things to look at all around the room. This is where we do Art. There's so much to see that it is hard for me to pay attention to the teacher, but I like to cut and paste. I feel special when Mama puts my art on the refrigerator.

There is a special room for Science class. It is really hard for me to pay attention. I learn best when I can see what is being taught, and I really like when we get to go outside to look at trees, bugs and plants.

Recess is a great time for me to let out my energy. Swinging helps to calm me down, but sometimes I just prefer to run, while maybe flapping my arms or tapping my hands, or climb. I might even try to play tag with my classmates.

Once a week I get to check out a new book from the school library. My Para helps me find a book I would like to take home. I like books that I can memorize, especially rhyming books, and pictures help me remember what the words are.

I really enjoy the computer. At home, Mama lets me on the computer when my homework is done or I've been a good boy. At school, I get to use the computer to learn. There are some websites that read stories to me and show pictures from books that Mama can buy for me.

I made it through another full day of school. I'm ready for the bus driver to take me home to Mama. She can read my journal notes, talk with me about my day, and help me with my homework so I'm ready to come back tomorrow.

www.ingramcontent.com/pod-product-compliance
Lightning Source LLC
Chambersburg PA
CBHW060828290526

45792CB00005BB/1841